THE BEAT

NOW

LES.

AND THEN

PHOTOGRAPHS BY

HARRY BENSON

UNIVERSE

I would like to dedicate the book to my children,
Tessa and Wendy.

﹏ ACKNOWLEDGMENTS

I would like to thank the Beatles for the privilege of photographing them; Antonio Polito
and Charles Miers of Universe for publishing this book; Bonnie Eldon and Ilaria Fusina
for their help in editing; Mirko Ilić and So Takahashi for the design; photographers David
Cairns and Jonathan Delano; Benjamina Baron; Cara Sutherland and the Newseum;
Canon, U.S.A.; and my wife, Gigi, without whom this book would not have happened.

Edited by Gigi Benson.
Back Cover: Suffolk Downs Race Track, Boston, August 18, 1966.

First published in the United States of America in 1998
by UNIVERSE PUBLISHING
A Division of Rizzoli International Publications, Inc.
300 Park Avenue South New York, NY 10010

98 99 00 01 02 / 10 9 8 7 6 5 4 3 2 1

Library of Congress Cataloging Card Number: 98-60895
Design:Mirko Ilić Corp.
Printed in Singapore

CONTENTS

⤳ PAUL McCARTNEY

To me, **PAUL** was the leader of the band. **PAUL** was also the kindest one. He would always find time to talk to the fans, the reporters, whoever. He would make people laugh. Stopping, talking, and signing autographs, he would always be the last to leave. If there was a decision to be made **JOHN** looked to **PAUL** for confirmation. Decisions were definitely made by the two of them, but they took pains not to show the outside world they were in charge.

∿ GEORGE HARRISON

I was actually closer to **GEORGE** than to the other three. We went out to clubs sometimes and I always sat and talked with **GEORGE** much more than I did with the others. **JOHN** used to talk about intellectuals he had met; **PAUL** liked to talk about the movie stars he'd met; and **RINGO** talked about the royalty who had come to meet them. **GEORGE** talked about Segovia, the great Spanish guitarist. "I'll never be as great as he is," he said, "but that's what I'm aiming for."

It's interesting that the one song on the *Rubber Soul* album written by **GEORGE** was titled "Think for Yourself." He was quietly determined to keep his integrity.

✍ RINGO STARR

RINGO was not sophisticated at all at first. You can see in some of the pictures that he really deferred to **JOHN** and **PAUL**.

I remember asking Duke Ellington once who the most important person in a band was and he said definitely the drummer. A bad drummer can throw off the rest of the band. Ellington said he didn't care about the drummer's personality: he could be the man in the moon, as long as he could drum. Everything comes from that beat. **RINGO** was not the man in the moon—he was a streetwise kid from Liverpool who could drum. He was rough around the edges but he learned quickly.

∽ JOHN LENNON

JOHN was very natural and naturally intelligent. He was funny too, always making cryptic jokes that made us laugh. He loved to order room service everywhere they stayed—they all did.

The last time I saw JOHN was from a distance at an anti-Vietnam War peace rally in Bryant Park in New York City in the late sixties, where he said, "All we're saying is give peace a chance." I knew the State Department would try to deport him. He did all he could to stay in the United States and eventually it was alright, but it was very, very close.

Photograph by Bill Epperidge © 1964

INTRODUCTION

As a young photojournalist I was assigned to photograph **THE BEATLES** on their first trip to Paris in 1964 and I wasn't keen on it at first. I was all set to go to Kenya to document the first anniversary of the country's independence, which was a big assignment at the time, while **THE BEATLES** were still relatively unknown, just breaking into the music scene. But before I left for Africa I was told to drop everything and go to Paris.

A Manchester newspaper reporter named Derek Taylor whom **THE BEATLES** liked and trusted introduced me to them. There had been another London newspaper photographer on the assignment in England, but the band didn't like him because they said he was ugly. The worst thing you could be around the four of them was ugly.

The first time I heard them play was in a little place on the outskirts of Paris. They started singing "All My Loving" and I really thought it was wonderful. It was the first song of theirs I heard and it will always be my definitive **BEATLES** song.

When they walked out onstage, I remember **PAUL** saying something like, "This is our first trip to Paris, give us your support." But they didn't need any, they took the audience by storm.

The press loved **THE BEATLES**; they were enormously quick-witted, always a good story, and arguably the most popular group ever. Before I met them in Paris I didn't really care if I did the story or not, but when I heard the music I changed my mind. It didn't take long to figure out that they were a phenomenon. Looking back on my career, there are some stories I'd love to go back and do better, but not **THE BEATLES**—I know I covered them to the best of my ability.

I remember that **GEORGE** used to say he never expected to make any money with the band—just enough to open a little business. Six, seven months, that's what he thought it would be because rock groups come and go so quickly. **RINGO** wanted to open a hair dresser's. They weren't sure it was going to last. Supremely confident, **JOHN** said he always felt that success was a matter of time. **PAUL**, ever aware of their image, was determined to get ahead.

By 1967, when the album *Sergeant Pepper's Lonely Hearts Club Band* was released, **THE BEATLES** and I had gone our separate ways. I became more involved with American assignments and I began to cover the civil rights marches, the riots, and the political scene. In 1969, Yoko and **JOHN**, and **PAUL** and Linda married; in 1970, **PAUL** announced that he was leaving **THE BEATLES**.

Now and then, over the ensuing years, I have photographed **PAUL** and Linda. The last time was at their farm in Peasmarsh, East Sussex, in 1992 (pages 6 to 9). Linda was riding her Appaloosa horse when **PAUL** joined us at the end of the day. I think these are my favorite photos of them together. Linda was always enthusiastic and full of life, and that is how I will remember her.

I have also photographed Yoko, Sean, and Julian, but I never had a chance to photograph **JOHN** again before he was killed, in 1980.

February 7, 1999, marks the 35th year since we all stepped off the plane onto the tarmac in New York for the first time (pages 2 and 3). Who could have known then what an impact these four men would have and continue to have today.

THE BEATLES not only changed the world, they changed my life as well. I never would have left Britain, nor been any kind of photographer if, by chance, I hadn't photographed them. Of course the assignment changed my life; I came to America with them and never went back. You can't change your life any more than that.

Photograph by Linda McCartney, taken with Harry Benson's camera, 1976.

♪ COMPOSING

I was in the sitting room of their suite in the George V Hotel in Paris in 1964. **PAUL** came in and was joined by **JOHN**. **RINGO** just slipped into the background as **PAUL** and **JOHN** sat down at the piano and started playing a few notes.

GEORGE came over with his guitar and began playing a few bars. They were very intense, completely absorbed in what they were doing. This went on for hours—they completely lost track of time; I had become invisible. They had already written a lot of great music, hits like "She Loves You" and "I Want to Hold Your Hand." As they played I heard

the melody first, then the words, "My baby's good to me, you know, she buys me diamond rings, you know." They were composing "I Feel Fine."

I am pleased with these pictures because there are not many photographs of **THE BEATLES** actually composing. Both **PAUL** and **JOHN** had very strong egos, very strong personalities, yet they respected one another. That is one reason they wrote great music together.

⚓ *PARIS*

We were on our way to the Olympia for the evening's performance on opening night. I wanted to get a photo before they went onstage and the best I could do was to get them all in a bar near the Olympia on the rue de la Paix.

Brian Epstein gave them the idea to dress alike. He wanted them to look nice and clean-cut. I know that JOHN was dead against it because he used to make comments about them being in monkey suits.

THE BEATLES went sightseeing on the Champs Elysées, not far from their
hotel. I wanted to get a picture of them on the streets of Paris, but it was so hard for them
to go anywhere without being overwhelmed by the fans. It was a cold day and it took some
time to get all four organized, but we went anyway.

They liked playing tourist and seeing a few of the sights. They all had cameras and they
all liked taking pictures, even if it was only of each other.

ꙮ NAPOLEON

One of the waiters said to **JOHN** in broken English that he reminded him of the Napoleon bust in the lobby of the George V Hotel. At the time, **PAUL** was considered the best looking of **THE BEATLES**, but I thought **JOHN** was—he had a refined nose, an uncommon face. Anyway, I photographed **JOHN** in front of the bust of Napoleon and had the rest of them line up.

☙ ON STAGE

At the Olympia, every performance was sold out. As soon as the curtain went up and **THE BEATLES** began to sing, the audience was theirs—mesmerized. They had fun on stage; they didn't talk very much in between songs. They just played and sang, song after song.

THE BEATLES always bowed after every song. At the gig outside Paris, and at the Olympia, they did their deep bow. Epstein told them to bow from the waist, but they didn't like it; later, they stopped doing it. They had a very different act from the Elvis Presley kind of filling-station sexiness.

✒ FAN MAIL

They had just gotten up when this picture was taken, at about three or four in the after-noon. A huge pile of fan mail had just arrived. They all sat around going through the let-ters and the packages addressed to each of them. JOHN was the most handsome in the classic sense, but I think I would have a lot of women arguing with me on that. PAUL had a cute face, and GEORGE was nice looking, but RINGO, I believe, received the most fan mail. Women seemed to think their chances were better with RINGO.

Fans sent them a lot of presents, too. If someone sent three of one thing and there wasn't a fourth, the one that was left out would sulk. A lot of the presents were girls' pictures; cheap and silly things, idiotic rubbish like plastic swords, whistles, scarves, or games to play on the plane. But if there weren't four of them, the excluded one would go crazy. They would be grabbing things from one another, fighting over the toys. They were competitive over everything: women, attention, toys.

✍ PILLOW FIGHT

After one of the Paris shows at the Olympia, Brian Epstein came in at 3 A.M. to tell them that "I Want to Hold Your Hand" was the number one song in America and that they would be going there for the "Ed Sullivan Show" and their first American tour.

They felt caged up in their hotel after each of the performances they gave at the Olympia. There was a violent energy in them—this tremendous energy that had to be let out. They needed a way to let off steam. Security was very tight—Epstein especially was watching for any 13-year-old girls who might try to find their way into one of their rooms.

I had seen them have pillow fights before and when Brian Epstein left I said, "How about a pillow fight?" It became quite rough. They all seemed to take pleasure in hitting **PAUL** because he was acting a bit superior. It was quite funny and it went on for a long time because they were enjoying it so much. They were excited and happy about going to America.

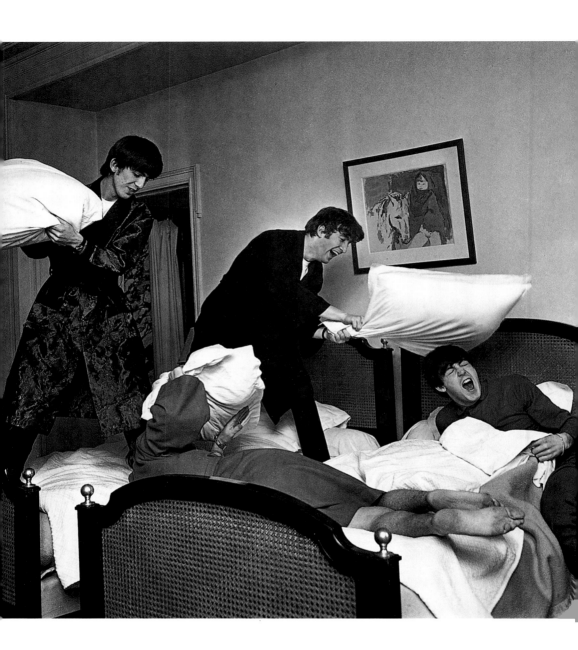

⤳ COMING TO AMERICA

On the plane coming to America for the first time, JOHN brought his first wife, Cynthia (Julian's mom). JOHN and Cynthia were really quiet on the plane. I wondered what effect having Cynthia along would have on the fans' reception.

On the plane, JOHN was complaining about some British photographers who, a few days earlier, had sneaked up on them and taken a picture of their baby, Julian. JOHN was annoyed by that. To me, it was just the beginning of what was going to become his life.

To pass the time, they took turns photographing each other. PAUL was trying to sleep on the plane so he put a napkin over his head. He had been out very late the night before with model-actress Jane Asher, who was his girlfriend at the time.

As the plane got closer, they became more and more excited about arriving. There was a naiveté about them; a playfulness that emerged. They were so young—none of the world-weariness had set in. This was their time.

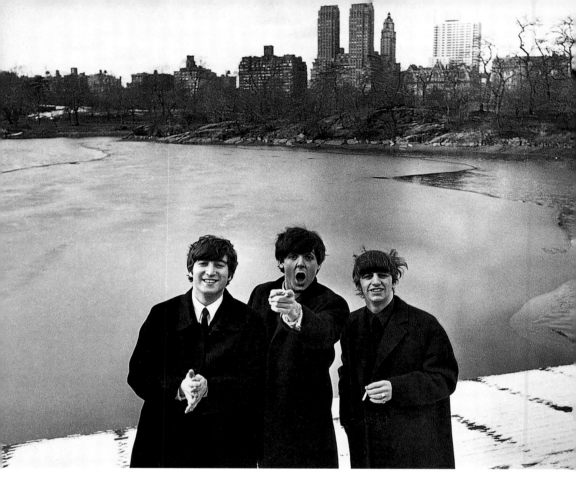

⌁ NEW YORK

Because **GEORGE** was in bed with a sore throat, it was just **JOHN**, **PAUL**, and **RINGO** who visited Central Park in New York City. Their faces were youthful, happy— not jaded. Afterwards, as their lifestyles changed, they looked different.

I had wanted to photograph them on the Brooklyn Bridge with the Manhattan skyline in the background, but it was an extremely cold day so we stayed close to the hotel. Iron- ically, I had to settle for Central Park with the West Side skyline, including the Dakota apartment building, where **JOHN** would later live and die.

With the sudden success of "I Want To Hold Your Hand," everybody in the U.S. wanted to talk to them; to meet them.

In between giving interviews, rehearsing for the "Ed Sullivan Show," and preparing for two concerts at Carnegie Hall, they found time just to play around. I asked the American photographers what they thought of **THE BEATLES**. They had seen everyone from Castro to royalty come and go, and **THE BEATLES** had caused more commotion than most. These were the jaded New York press guys, the ones who wore their press cards in their hats—even they were impressed.

✎ ED SULLIVAN

On the plane to New York they kept saying, "We're going to meet Ed Sullivan, Ed Sullivan." He was like the Pope to them. They always addressed him as "Mister Sullivan." They knew just what he was doing for their career.

We left the Plaza Hotel with swarms of fans outside. The good-humored New York City policemen were there trying to keep order. "We see them!" cried the girls outside as we rushed to the limo on the way to the "Ed Sullivan Show".

The five of us were crunched into the back of the limousine. The fans had been waiting a long time outside in the cold and the girls rushed up to the windows screaming. I was there to see it from **THE BEATLES'** perspective—to be at the center.

What's interesting about **THE BEATLES** is that this phenomenon had never happened before. Elvis and Sinatra had been idols in their day, but they were singers, they didn't compose their own music.

Ed Sullivan even got a **BEATLES'** wig from someone in the audience and he put it on his head while warming up the crowd before the show. Girls in the audience were crying, screaming, fainting, jumping up and down—it was bedlam. It was estimated that over 73 million people watched the show, one of the largest TV audiences ever.

≫ MIAMI

At the airport, local beauty pageant winners met them coming off the plane and followed them wherever they went—even to the beach. To say that a lot of women were interested in meeting **THE BEATLES** would be a gross understatement.

In Florida, the crowds were calm. I wanted to photograph **THE BEATLES** on the beach and they obliged. They were all wearing the same thing. I think someone had sent over matching terry cloth cover-up outfits for them and they all put them on. The girls on the beach were shy but curious. You could never take photographs like that now. Rock stars of this magnitude would be surrounded by bodyguards today.

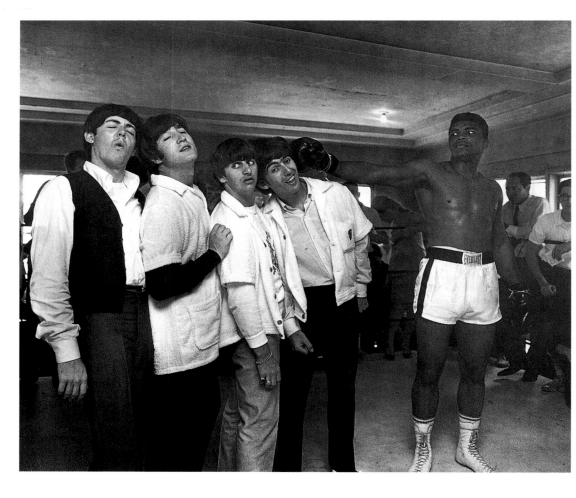

≈ CASSIUS CLAY

In Florida, **THE BEATLES** said they wanted to meet the world heavyweight champion Sonny Liston. This was before the famous Clay-Liston match. Liston told me that he didn't want to see the "bums" so I had to quickly substitute the challenger, Cassius Clay. It was only later, after he beat Liston, that Clay changed his name to Muhammad Ali.

We went down to the ring and Clay ordered the Beatles around telling them to lie down, line up, etc. He called **PAUL** the pretty one, but told him, "You're not as pretty as me." Clay was great. **THE BEATLES** played along, but they looked stunned when

they walked out. They weren't happy because for the first time someone else had taken over. They had been acting really cocky and funny in their press conferences. They thought they were going to meet some dumb boxer and when they met Clay, they were really thrown for a loop. They felt taken advantage of, and wouldn't speak to me for a few days. Afterwards, **JOHN** said, "That man made a fool of us." It wasn't pleasant having **THE BEATLES** mad at me, especially **JOHN**.

✍ AMSTERDAM AND COPENHAGEN

The message came over the wire service that **RINGO** was ill. There was speculation about whether or not their spring 1964 tour of Holland and Denmark would be canceled.

Instead of canceling they got Jimmy Nichol, another drummer, to stand in on the trip. He was a pleasant young man who was going to make the most of his days as a member of the most famous group in the world: he signed autographs and gave press interviews. Who could blame him? He was having a grand time, but the fans were disappointed that **RINGO** wasn't there.

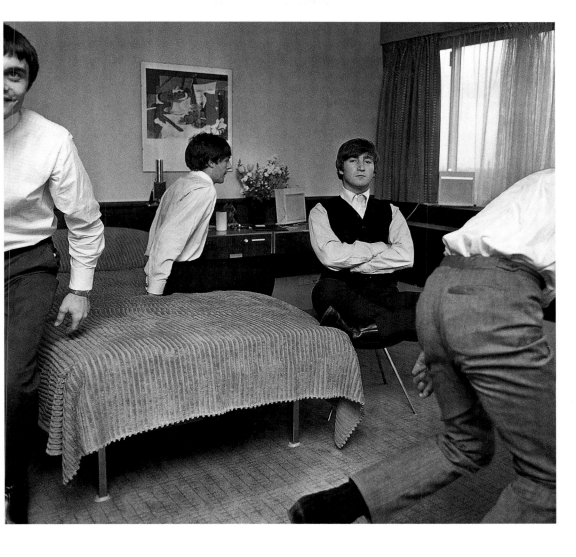

After Copenhagen **THE BEATLES** headed to Amsterdam, where they were scheduled to give a concert and appear live on Dutch TV.

The producers of the Dutch television show talked **THE BEATLES** into letting fans sit on the stage while they performed. They insisted it was safe, but what happened was that the producers arranged ahead of time to have the fans rush the band at the conclusion of their performance. Of course, it got a little bit out of hand. The fans rushed on while **THE BEATLES** were still singing and chaos ensued.

⌘ A HARD DAY'S NIGHT

Only five months after their appearance on the "Ed Sullivan Show," the band was filming *A Hard Day's Night*. They changed the name of the film after **RINGO** came in one morning, looking disheveled and hung over, and said, "It's been a hard day's night."

I spent a few days traveling on the train with them while they filmed. Director Richard Lester, character actor Wilfred Bramwell, and everyone on the set was amazed that they wrote the title song in one day.

When they were making the movie, people wondered what they'd be like in a film; they needn't have worried. The movie opened in July 1964 and was a smash hit. The critics said that although all four were good, **RINGO** was the most natural.

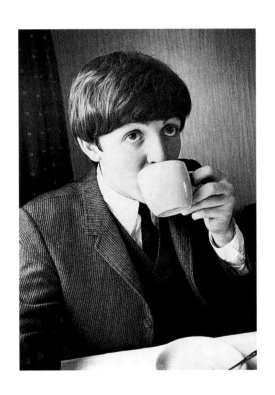

❧ HUSBANDS AND WIVES

GEORGE met Patti Boyd on the set of *A Hard Day's Night*. She was an extra and had a modeling career. When they married in 1966, their honeymoon location was kept secret. With a bit of detective work, though, I tracked them to Barbados. When we ran into each other, **GEORGE** thought it was a coincidence but I explained why I'd come and promised to let him get on with his honeymoon if he'd let me take a few pictures first. They were fine about it and we hung around together and had dinner that night.

After they divorced and she married Eric Clapton, **GEORGE** said he was glad Patti married Clapton instead of some jerk.

Maureen Cox and **RINGO** were married in 1965 in London, the year before **GEORGE** married Patti. Maureen and **RINGO** let me photograph them the day they got married. Both seemed very serene. They divorced in 1975, and **RINGO** has been married to actress Barbara Bach since 1981.

On their first American tour, **THE BEATLES** took the train from New York to Washington D.C. I remember Cynthia Lennon wore a black wig so as not to be recognized and mobbed by the fans.

✍ BEATLEMANIA

Beatlemania was escalating. I believe it was Derek Taylor, the correspondent from Manchester, who coined the word "Beatlemania." He later became **THE BEATLES'** road manager. Everywhere they performed there was mass hysteria. The minute they opened their mouths, the frenzy and screaming would start. They couldn't hear anything, so after a while they would start improvising and singing anything that came to mind. Fans threw shoes, coins, and paper cups at the stage; and **THE BEATLES** began to worry about getting hurt. They were beginning to tire of the madness of touring.

When **THE BEATLES'** music was played in a bar or pub people would get up and dance to it. People who were doing a slow waltz a week before were now dancing in a completely new way. Everything changed. It was a phenomenon. People changed their hair, their clothes. Everyone wanted to be like them. Kings of exotic foreign countries were asking if they could meet them. **THE BEATLES** were beginning to like this newfound celebrity.

Lots of people even began copying how they spoke. People from the middle and upper classes in England started speaking with ridiculous Liverpool street accents because of **THE BEATLES**. It was becoming infectious.

✑ PRESS CONFERENCE

THE BEATLES generated mass hysteria everywhere they went. They were care-free and always clowning around. I think part of the reason they were so appealing is that they were what everyone wanted to be: young, witty, and full of talent.

At press conferences in 1966, if someone asked **THE BEATLES** a smart-ass question, they would put them in their place. It was a mistake to ask something like, "Do you have any conscience about corrupting the youth of America?" because they always had a quick retort. No one asked them that kind of question twice.

~ CHICAGO

JOHN gave an interview to English journalist Maureen Cleave, in which he said that the BEATLES' were more popular than Jesus. It caused quite an uproar. I was somewhere else on another story and was told to get to Chicago as quickly as I could. JOHN was very upset and started to sob, saying, "Why did I open my big mouth, why did I do it? I didn't mean it." And the rest of the BEATLES were really quite annoyed with him. He issued a formal apology retracting his statement.

People in the Bible belt were burning BEATLES records. It was a very serious thing; people were calling radio talk shows condemning the band. D.J.'s across the country were keeping count of the number of stores that refused to sell their records and announcing the results on the air. This went on for weeks. At a concert in Chicago, the police lined up in front of the stage to protect THE BEATLES from the threats of outraged fans. Even a later concert at Shea Stadium wasn't sold out because of JOHN'S statement—about 10,000 seats were left empty.

At the time JOHN was not cocky about it, although he was later. Of course, some people think he was right.

On December 14, 1989, at JOHN'S Central Park memorial service, emotional fans carried candles, flowers, and pictures of him. They played his music, cried, hugged, and mourned the loss of a legend.

WINGS

∾ WINGS

Traveling with the Wings band on their plane in 1976 was like old times. Band members Joe English, drums; Jimmy McCulloch, lead guitar; and Denny Laine, rhythm guitar; joined Linda and **PAUL** to make up the band.

Backstage at the end of a concert in Philadelphia, they were tired and sweaty, weary but happy. They visited with friends and relaxed before leaving for the next stop on their tour.

PAUL in the control room of the recording studio in Los Angeles, listened intently to the final playback of one of the songs for the new album.

When **PAUL** walked out on stage, the fans turned on their small flashlights and the whole auditorium was like a sea of sparkling lights. At the end of a song, he lifted his guitar the same way as I'd seen him do so many times before.

➷ THE McCARTNEYS

When the photographs of **PAUL**, Linda, and the children were taken in 1975, they were in California for **PAUL** to record a new album for Wings.

Linda's twelve-year-old daughter, Heather, whom **PAUL** adopted, and their five-year-old, Mary, happily posed, but Stella, three at the time, had her doubts. Stella, now the Paris-based designer for Chloé, has received rave reviews from the critics a well as from her proud parents. Stella's collection, shown in early 1998, was one of Linda's last public appearances, and she seemed so happy about Stella's success.

Sitting next to **PAUL** at the piano in the California home they were leasing, Stella sat very still and watched intently as **PAUL** played and sang to her.

"My family is my life," **PAUL** said, and breakfast was family time. Mary had lost her front teeth and enjoyed making her father laugh by making funny faces.

～ PARTY ON THE Q.E. II

The Queen Elizabeth II, dry-docked near Long Beach, California, was the setting for the *Venus and Mars* album's wrap party in 1975. Among the 300 guests were **GEORGE** and Olivia Arias, who would marry in 1978. It was good to see him again. Bob Dylan also made a rare appearance.

PAUL and Linda danced and greeted all their guests and seemed to have the best time of all. The ballroom was star-studded. Everyone from Cher to Tatum O'Neal danced the night away. **PAUL** and Linda took to the floor and broke out into an exuberant dance of their own. The relief of having finished the album was clearly cause for celebration.

♫ IMAGINE

The first time I met Yoko Ono was in 1985. I went to the Dakota where she and Sean live and where JOHN had been killed in 1980. I found her to be a smart, down-to-earth woman. Yoko and Sean played the piano, sang, and played a game of chess. Then we went across the street to Central Park. They sat in Strawberry Fields at the Imagine Circle, ran, and played tag. It seemed Yoko had decided to remember JOHN in a positive way, knowing that JOHN would have wanted that for Sean.

I photographed Julian Lennon when he came to New York in late 1984 to publicize his first album, *Valotte*. He, like Sean, bears a striking resemblance to his father.

In 1990, I photographed them again at Yoko's home in Switzerland. I was surprised at how tall Sean had become, and Yoko stood on the bed to be taller than he was.

Yoko and Sean were recording in Manhattan in 1995 and took time out to let me photograph them. Sean is now a talented musician in his own right. I photographed the two of them again in the New York studio in 1996 where they were recording with Sean's band.

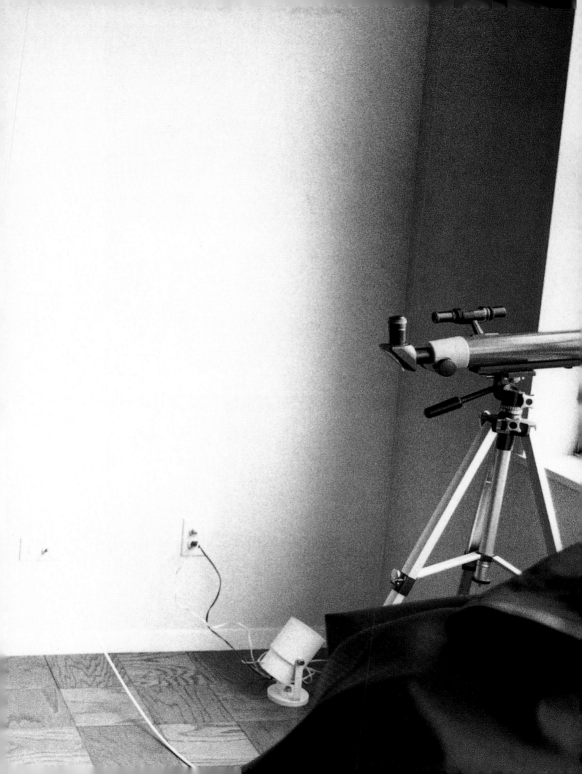